THE UNSIGNIFICANT

SRIKANTH REDDY

THE
UNSIGNIFICANT

Three Talks on Poetry and Pictures

WAVE BOOKS

SEATTLE AND NEW YORK

Published by Wave Books

www.wavepoetry.com

Copyright © 2024 by Srikanth Reddy

Wave Books titles are distributed to the trade by

Consortium Book Sales and Distribution

Phone: 800-283-3572 / SAN 631-760X

Library of Congress Cataloging-in-Publication Data

Names: Reddy, Srikanth, 1973– author.

Title: The unsignificant : three talks on poetry and pictures / Srikanth Reddy.

Description: First edition. | Seattle : Wave Books, 2024. |

Series: Bagley Wright lecture series | Includes bibliographical references.

Identifiers: LCCN 2024009230 | ISBN 9798891060067 (paperback)

Subjects: LCSH: Poetry. | Poetics. | LCGFT: Lectures. | Literary criticism.

Classification: LCC PN1031 .R386 2024 | DDC 808.1—dc23/eng/20240305

LC record available at https://lccn.loc.gov/2024009230

Image credits: *Landscape with the Fall of Icarus* (p. 7) by Pieter Bruegel, *Soap Bubbles* (p. 9) by Jean Siméon Chardin, reflectography detail (p. 17) via MRBAB/photo by KIK-IRPA © Bruxelles, Inkblot #2 (p. 20) by Hermann Rorschach, photograph of Rorschach in 1910 (p. 21), *Chaos* (p. 32) by Maestro Bartolomé, *Chaos* (p. 33) by Takashi Murakami, *The Poet* (p. 34) by Pablo Picasso, *Portrait of Dante Alighieri* (p. 39) by Gustave Doré, *The Shield of Achilles* (p. 50) designed by John Flaxman and cast by Rundell & Bridge, *Fifty Days at Iliam: Shield of Achilles* (p. 51) by Cy Twombly, sketch of the moon (p. 57) by Galileo Galilei from *Sidereus Nuncius*, *Three representations of the moon* (p. 58) by Claude Mellan, Moon globe (p. 59) by John Russell, erasure of John Milton's *Paradise Lost* (p. 63) by Ronald Johnson, pages from 1977 Sand Dollar edition of *Radi Os* (p. 64, 72) by Ronald Johnson, page from 1892 Thomas Y. Crowell edition of *Paradise Lost* (p. 67/68).

Designed by Crisis

Printed in the United States of America

9 8 7 6 5 4 3 2 1

First Edition

FOR FRANK BUFFAM

THE UNSIGNIFICANT

THE UNSIGNIFICANT

More often than not, as any analyst will tell you, the background is as important as the foreground in looking at things. I, for one, can only contemplate so many crucifixions before my eyes start wandering toward the two thieves in their supporting predicaments in Rembrandt's *Three Crosses*, or the porter in an ivory turban carrying off a ladder stage left in van der Weyden's *Abegg Triptych*, or the incongruous windmill perched on a faraway hilltop in Bosch's *Crucifixion with a Donor*. I may be moved in any number of ways by a figure in the foreground, but it's only a picture's background that can really *absorb* me. So I was a little disappointed when, preparing for this talk, I failed to unearth a single treatise on the subject of backgrounds in the history of art. I began to wonder whether this missing background had something to do with the nature of background itself. Maybe nobody foregrounds backgrounds for a reason.

I found myself wondering, what is a background? Is it just a figure suffering from low self-esteem? What are we missing when we disregard those unassuming little figures—birds, clouds, unmanned military drones —in the offing? Can paying attention to what's going on in the background make you a better person? Can we see—or hear, or smell, or taste, or touch—anything whatsoever without some sort of negative space behind, or around, or before and after it? And, because I spend too much of my time thinking about poetry, I also wondered, what can poems tell us about the background of things?

One way of answering this last question may be to look at W. H. Auden looking into the background. In the December of 1938, Auden was in transit, holed up in Belgium after six months spent touring the Second Sino-Japanese War with his companion Christopher Isherwood. During his time in China, Auden had visited hospitals overflowing with the dying and dead, sipped tea with expatriates during a Japanese air raid, made several Chaplinesque attempts to reach the front line, and was christened with the phonetic Chinese name "Au Dung," which he later printed on his business cards. A bloody conflict on the far side of the planet was in the background of Auden's consciousness, then, when he viewed a series of paintings by Pieter Bruegel the Elder at the Palais des Beaux-Arts one winter day in Brussels before the outbreak of World War II. The poem commemorating this encounter, "Musée des Beaux Arts," is one of Auden's most widely anthologized poems, and probably the most famous example of ekphrasis in modern Anglophone verse. But "Musée des Beaux Arts" is not so much a poem about a particular painting as it is a meditation on the suffering that goes unnoticed in the background of ordinary experience:

> About suffering they were never wrong,
> The Old Masters: how well they understood
> Its human position; how it takes place
> While someone else is eating or opening a window or just walking dully along;
> How, when the aged are reverently, passionately waiting
> For the miraculous birth, there always must be
> Children who did not specially want it to happen, skating
> On a pond at the edge of the wood:

They never forgot
That even the dreadful martyrdom must run its course
Anyhow in a corner, some untidy spot
Where the dogs go on with their doggy life and the torturer's horse
Scratches its innocent behind on a tree.

I must admit that I'm not particularly enamored of the speaker in this poem. Beginning with his preposterous proclamation that the Old Masters were "never" wrong about suffering, this character sounds like one of those pedantic museum guides who are rarely at a loss for magisterial declarations about high art. You can almost picture him walking backward through the gallery as he gesticulates toward various canvases with a mannered poetical "how": "how well they understood," "how it takes place," "how . . . there always must be," and, later, "how everything turns away." Nevertheless, our guide adroitly points out noteworthy details in the margins of paintings, from the children skating "at the edge" of a wood to the martyrdom that must run its feverish course "in a corner" of another composition. This is the "human position" of suffering in the Old Masters' world: not in the foreground, but rather off in a corner at the edge of perception.

Misery, says the museum guide, is a matter of optics. While my pain may seem monumental to me, from another person's perspective it is little more than a trivial background detail. After the stanza break, Auden's speaker pauses before one painting that spectacularly illustrates our habitual disregard for distant figures of affliction:

In Breughel's *Icarus*, for instance: how everything turns away
Quite leisurely from the disaster; the ploughman may
Have heard the splash, the forsaken cry,

3

But for him it was not an important failure; the sun shone
As it had to on the white legs disappearing into the green
Water; and the expensive delicate ship that must have seen
Something amazing, a boy falling out of the sky,
Had somewhere to get to and sailed calmly on.

The ploughman ignores Icarus's cry because, for him, the boy's fall is not an "important failure," like the failure of crops, or of markets, or of one's own heart. But the ploughman isn't the only indifferent figure in this picture. It's one thing to say that everyone ignores the disaster, and another matter entirely to say "every*thing* turns away," as if every inch of the canvas recoiled from the sinkhole of Icarus's calamity. Almost reluctantly, the painted sun shines "as it had to" on Icarus's fallen figure, and this lack of celestial sympathy is paralleled by the mercantile disregard of the "expensive delicate ship" that sails off at the poem's conclusion. Auden artfully registers three kinds of indifference toward suffering in this stanza: human indifference (the ploughman), environmental indifference (the sun), and artifactual indifference (the ship). "Musée des Beaux Arts" brings these dimensions together into an ingenious little theater of obliviousness. The "important failure" in the poem is a universal failure—of ploughman, sun, and ship alike—to register the suffering of others.

And yet, if "Musée des Beaux Arts" were simply a poem about cosmic heartlessness, it wouldn't be quite so interesting as a work of art. Instead, Auden quietly changes his mind about what's going on in the background as his poem unfolds. "Suffering" was never a very good word for Icarus's predicament, after all. Suffering, like any art, takes time. The boy's father, Daedalus, suffers the misery of outliving his child, but Icarus himself doesn't *suffer* so much as he experiences some other more sudden and terrible affect, like horror or dismay, before plunging into the waves below. Though his story is frequently invoked as a parable of vaulting ambition, or filial disobedience, or any number of other object lessons, I sometimes think nobody will ever understand poor Icarus. Even the Hellenic Air Force Academy, which really ought to know better, claims the falling boy for its emblem, proudly emblazoning its cadets' badges with a winged youth forever transfixed by the sun's rays.

It adds a fatalistic air to that institution's oddly wistful motto: "We shall become much better than you."

By the poem's second stanza, our museum guide senses that Icarus won't fit comfortably into his general discourse on suffering—so he shiftily changes course, now referring to the boy's fate as "the disaster." Disaster is much better, in an Elizabeth Bishop sort of way, than suffering as a description of Icarus's fall. (We'll come back to disaster a little later in this talk.) And yet Auden's re-examination of the boy in the background doesn't stop here, either. A few lines later, the poem revises its own blind spot yet again, no longer describing Icarus's fate as disastrous, but rather as "something *amazing*." This final perspective on Icarus's calamity might seem amoral, or even immoral, to somebody seeking a moral to the poem. When you stop to think about it, though, every disaster—this earthquake, that heartbreak—*does* amaze us. At the heart of Auden's word, "amazing," is the maze that Icarus's father devised to confine the Minotaur—a labyrinth that might have been lodged somewhere in the folds of the poet's brain when he wrote that plainspoken yet extraordinary line: "Something amazing, a boy falling out of the sky." The most amazing thing of all, Auden discovers, is that we do *not* lose ourselves in the labyrinthine background of our perceptual worlds. Only our ability to disregard what's in the offing—whether it be suffering, disaster, or even something amazing—permits us to sail, like a costly and fragile vessel, "calmly on."

II. SOME LESSER FIGURES

Today scholars think the unsigned and undated picture in the Palais des Beaux-Arts is most likely a copy after a lost original by Bruegel. Unbeknownst to him, Auden may have been viewing a picture painted by one of Bruegel's sons, or by one of those anonymous apprentices who devoted their talents to filling in the background details—foliage, distant citadels, a storm out the window—of paintings signed by their more famous masters. My own theory is that the picture was painted by Jorge Luis Borges in a previous life. It's a work of art that keeps turning itself inside out. Even the grammar of the painting's title, *Landscape with the Fall of Icarus*, oddly reflects the reversal of figure and ground that we see

6

worked out in the composition of the canvas itself. (Though it's changed names a few times over the centuries, art historians generally go with *Landscape with the Fall of Icarus* today.) A sixteenth-century viewer would have expected Icarus's tragic figure to occupy center stage, with details like clouds, ships, and coast filling in the painting's background. Here, however, we find a landscape—the classic genre of pictorial distances—front and center, with poor little Icarus downsized to a recessed detail in the composition. Not "The Fall of Icarus with Landscape," then, but *Landscape with the Fall of Icarus.*

One background may hide another; glimpsed through the scrim of Auden's text, *Landscape with the Fall of Icarus* conceals yet another, much older, poem behind it. The painting turns ekphrasis itself inside out, visually illustrating a literary passage in Ovid's *Metamorphoses* where the sea swallows Daedalus's son:

> *Oraque caerulea patrium clamantia nomen*
> *excipiuntur aqua, quae nomen traxit ab illo.*

> And his mouth, calling his father's name, was engulfed
> by the cerulean sea that draws its name from him.

With a signature flourish, Ovid folds an origami figure of orality and absorption into the prosodic envelope of these two hexameters. Here the sea swallows the little opening of Icarus's mouth as a synecdoche for his corporeal being. Icarus, in turn, must swallow the fatal waters that flood into his throat as he calls his father's name. In the end, though, the devouring sea is subsumed by the drowned boy's identity, as its waters are henceforward named after him. An anonymous sea becomes the Icarian Sea. *Landscape with the Fall of Icarus* visualizes the precise moment of this mutual absorption of boy by sea and sea by boy. Indeed, the whole of the *Metamorphoses* can be read as an elaborate pageantry of figures that emerge only to be absorbed, inexorably, into the artwork's background— a girl turns into a tree, a boy changes into a flower, a queen becomes a constellation, and so on.

Icarus isn't the only figure of absorption on display in this painting. The farmer bends over his plough, thoroughly engrossed by his work. The hunched fisherman fixes his gaze on the inscrutable bottle-green waters before him. Ignoring his flock, the shepherd peers upward at the missing portion of the canvas where Daedalus sails forever into his own grief overhead. Ovid imagines these bystanders watching, amazed, as Icarus and his father fly like gods through his poem; but in the painting's *optical* regime, nobody notices the falling boy. If Icarus is physically absorbed into the sea that furnishes a deep background to *Landscape with the Fall of Icarus*, the painting's other figures display a *mental* absorption in the immediate objects of their attention: the soil underfoot, the waters ahead, the superintending sky. The art historian Michael Fried has argued that such scenes of mental absorption—a girl reading a book, for example, or a boy constructing a house of cards—go on to become the fundamental subject, or "master configuration," of eighteenth-century French painting.

The individuals depicted in these images are so entranced by their own preoccupations that they seem to flagrantly *disregard* their beholder:

> For French painters of the early and mid-1750s the persuasive representation of absorption entailed evoking the perfect obliviousness of a figure or group of figures to everything but the objects of their absorption. *Those objects did not include the beholder standing before the painting.* Hence the figure or figures had to seem oblivious to the beholder's presence if the illusion of absorption was to be sustained.

The ploughman, the shepherd, and the fisherman in *Landscape with the Fall of Icarus* are each, in their own way, oblivious to the beholder's presence. They presage the eighteenth-century tradition that Fried so brilliantly investigates. But why should these bit players from Ovid ignore the viewer as if you or I were insignificant bystanders in the background of their lives? Their stubborn absorption verges on insolence. Fried explains that gazing back at the beholder might somehow dislodge these characters from the order of the world they inhabit:

> It is as though the presence of the beholder threatened to distract the dramatis personae from all involvement in ordinary states and activities, and as though the artist was therefore called upon to neutralize the beholder's presence by taking whatever measures proved necessary to absorb, or reabsorb, those personae in the world of the painting.

Fried's theses on absorption open up an entirely new way of reading "Musée des Beaux Arts." When we first come across the phrase "everything turns away / quite leisurely from the disaster" in the poem, we take the disaster to be synonymous with Icarus himself. And of course, the ploughman, the shepherd, and the fisherman do turn away from the boy's flailing limbs in the painting—but they also decline, quite conspicuously, to look at *me*. Could I be the disaster? I am, it appears, what everyone in the painting must disregard if their world is to hold itself together. It's nothing personal, of course, since anybody—W. H. Auden, a Greek air force cadet, you, me, or even Michael Fried—ought to feel the same way standing before the painting: *I am the disaster*. Dis, from the Greek prefix *dys*, meaning "bad" or "ill," and aster, from *astron*, denoting a "planet" or "star." The sense is astrological, of a calamity caused by the unfavorable position of a celestial body. We are all bad planets circling the pictured worlds that we behold.

Sometimes I feel a little dizzy when I look at this painting. Fried might call it an absorption problem. It all begins with that uncomfortably crowded foreground, where every figure seems slightly off-balance. See how the ploughman's right foot rhymes with the precariously planted rear hoof of his horse as they both tread the uneven edge of the furrow they cut? I worry, also, about the shepherd with his head thrown back in reverie, oblivious to the nasty little drop just a step or two behind him. We mustn't forget the fisherman either, recklessly shifting his center of balance as he casts his line out over the engulfing waters. I, too, am put in an awkward position by this pictorial contraption—invisibly perched on a raised ledge looking over the foreground toward an airy maritime panorama. Even the horizon, placed quite high in the composition (as it is so often in Bruegel's work), makes me feel as if the whole terrain were tilting upward, the floor underfoot becoming a wall before me, so that I'm gazing down on the landscape rather than out across it. It's the perspective of somebody about to launch themselves on a risky flight: an Icarian perspective.

The whole visual logic of the composition gives me the sensation of being next in line to share the falling boy's disaster, like some sort of existential lemming poised to tumble, in turn, over the edge of the painting's frame. This might be why the sea fills up so much of the picture's volume, stretching itself out in a voluptuous recession that reveals the curvature of the planet in its engrossing surface. Like the sea it so luxuriantly depicts, *Landscape with the Fall of Icarus* is a kind of absorption machine. The anonymous figures in the foreground may presage an Enlightenment tradition of mannered disregard, but Icarus belongs to an earlier, more violent moment in the history of pictorial absorption. Unlike the ploughman, the shepherd, and the fisherman, Icarus cannot survive his own absorption because it claims not only his seeing, but his entire being as well. It isn't phenomenological, so to speak, but ontological. The sinister aspect of this visual system—see that blade pointing out from the lower left corner of the canvas?—emerges from our sense that we, too, risk something by our absorption in its pictured world.

Every time we see a figure in the background, we become a kind of Icarus writ small. In his book *Phenomenology of Perception*, the philosopher Maurice Merleau-Ponty describes his sense of engulfment in another person's perspective:

> *A vortex forms around the perceived body into which my world is drawn and, so to speak, sucked in*: to this extent, my world is no longer merely mine, it is no longer present only to me, it is present to X, to this other behavior that begins to take shape in it. The other body is already no longer a simple fragment of the world, but rather the place of a certain elaboration and somehow a certain "view" of the world.

Far from being objects of idle indifference, background figures exert a discombobulating kind of perspectival suction on the beholder. Viewing somebody from afar entails knowing that they, too, entertain a perspective on the world—a view from which you yourself are but a background detail. The imagery of the whirlpool conveys the psychological vertigo that accompanies this recognition. Merleau-Ponty's vortex is the troubled water where Icarus vanishes. We may respond to this vortex in different ways—by turning away, by plunging in, by fixing our gaze on its whirling surface—but every response discloses our attitude toward a perceptual background that is the foreground of other lives.

We've observed how the ploughman, the shepherd, and the fisherman display what might be called a phenomenological absorption within the world of the painting. They appear to be wholly engrossed by the objects of their attention, blinding them to both Icarus's disaster and our own. And we've seen how Icarus is ontologically absorbed into the background of this pictured world. He bequeaths his identity to the sea that engulfs him. Neither alternative—obliviousness nor annihilation—sounds very appealing to me. But there is a third possibility open to us as well, and before I run out of fancy words, I'll propose that we call it *epistemological* absorption. Unlike the ploughman, the shepherd, or the fisherman—who gaze at the earth, the sky, and the water, respectively—we ourselves do not fixate on only *one* Heraclitean element in the world of the picture. We examine the whole structure, studying how it works, in order to understand what kind of knowledge it has to offer us. What do we learn from this inside-out picture of the world? As if we were watching a play from backstage, we see what things look like when background and foreground change places. Supporting actors perform leading roles, and stars become supernumeraries. The name of this absorbing comedy is *The Human Position*.

III. UNSIGNIFICANCE

In the spring of 1960—the year the Soviet Union shot down the American pilot Gary Powers as he skimmed the edge of the stratosphere in a U-2 reconnaissance plane—William Carlos Williams published his own variation on the fall of Icarus in *The Hudson Review*:

> According to Brueghel
> when Icarus fell
> it was spring
>
> a farmer was ploughing
> his field
> the whole pageantry
>
> of the year was
> awake tingling
> near
>
> the edge of the sea
> concerned
> with itself
>
> sweating in the sun
> that melted
> the wings' wax
>
> unsignificantly
> off the coast
> there was
>
> a splash quite unnoticed
> this was
> Icarus drowning

Like that little splash off the coast, this ekphrasis of *Landscape with the Fall of Icarus* has generally gone "quite unnoticed" by literary critics. Maybe it has something to do with the poem's prosody; measured against the rangy lines of "Musée des Beaux Arts," Williams seems to pursue his own brand of literary minimalism almost too successfully, to the edge of disappearance, in this work. But sometimes the longest word in a little poem can speak volumes. Here, the six syllables of "unsignificantly"— which I took as a typo for *insignificantly* the first time I read the poem— occupy a whole line unto themselves, ironically foregrounding the word's significance. Unsignificantly sounds almost right, but slightly off—not as bad as calling something "inimportant," but a shade more awkward than "unconsequential." Now obsolete, the word was an accepted variant of insignificance in seventeenth-century English usage, appearing, for example, in Milton's prose: "The temple of Janus with his two controversal faces might now not *unsignificantly* be set open." But I think Williams wants to do something more than just slip an outdated lexical variant into his poem with this repurposed prefix. The more you look into unsignificance, the more you will see there.

In an essay called "The Nature of Philosophy," Ludwig Wittgenstein writes that "the philosopher strives to find the liberating word, that is, the word which finally allows us to grasp what it is that has hitherto, imperceptibly, been a burden upon our consciousness." Unsignificance isn't a philosophical concept or term; it's a *poet's* liberating word for what imperceptibly burdens our consciousness. When we describe something as either significant or insignificant, we assign it a greater or lesser degree of importance. To call something unsignificant, though, is to suggest that it differs not in degree, but in kind. It doesn't signify—it *un*signifies. "It is like having a hair on your tongue," Wittgenstein continues parenthetically: "You feel it, but you can't get hold of it and get rid of it." This vexing elusiveness is reflected in the way that unsignificance seems to float free of reference in the unpunctuated grammar of Williams's poem. As his syntax unfolds, it initially sounds like the sun in the painting has "melted / the wings' wax // unsignificantly." But this doesn't seem right, since the painting itself wouldn't exist if the sun hadn't melted Icarus's wings in the first place. Maybe the stanza break nudges us to associate "unsignificantly" with the lines that immediately follow it instead:

> unsignificantly
> off the coast
> there was
>
> a splash quite unnoticed

This is better, though even here we'll still have to iron out a few readerly wrinkles. What exactly does the adverb "unsignificantly" modify in this sentence? It can't be the unnoticed splash, because "splash" is a noun. The only grammatical possibility, then, is the verb "was." So you could rewrite the sentence to read, "There was, unsignificantly, a quite unnoticed splash off the coast." Though the artist tucks this little splash of paint into an easily overlooked corner of the composition, its calculated placement there can hardly be described as insignificant. Yet nobody in the world of the painting—not even that tiny sailor, too busy with the ship's rigging to notice the feathers falling around him—finds the splash to be terribly significant either. Icarus falls into *unsignificance*. Looking on his splash's trace of signification, we participate in this plunge. We may even come to feel an inkling of our own unsignificance through our absorption in his little disaster.

Before closing, I'd like to dwell on one peculiar detail in this picture's background that has imperceptibly burdened the consciousness of art historians for nearly a century. At the edge of the ploughed field, directly above the horse's head, a man lies on his back in the undergrowth. You can make out his pale, upturned face sticking out of the dense brush like some ghostly afterimage from an earlier disaster. Many viewers have remarked upon the mystery of this "dead man" in the picture, but nobody has delivered him yet from the purgatory of unsignificance. One scholar proposes that the figure illustrates the Flemish proverb, "The plow does not stop on account of a dying man." Another points to the knife lying like a discarded murder weapon in the painting's lower left corner, implying some sort of allegorical foul play on the part of that shifty ploughman. Recently, infrared reflectography has given us some insight into the shadowy underdrawing beneath this curious detail.

Studying the netherworld below the painting's surface, the Belgian scholar Dominique Allart has arrived at the conclusion that this patch of mottled white is not a head at all, but quite the opposite. She discerns in its figure one of the earthier motifs of Northern European art: the bare bottom of a *kakkertje*, or, in English, a defecating man.

The community of Bruegel scholars has yet to weigh in on Allart's admittedly arguable view of things. For the time being, it remains a matter of heads or tails. But when I first caught wind of the *kakkertje*, there was no denying it—I believe in the defecating man. There he is, engaged in the most absorbing of human activities, or maybe the second most, depending on the state of one's love life. Nobody could be more oblivious toward Icarus, or toward us, for that matter. Yet on another level, the defecating man—or *my* defecating man, I should say—is forever captured in a state of incomplete absorption into the physical medium of the painting itself. He breaks through the unlit realm of the underdrawing to surface enigmatically in the painting's finish, like a petticoat about to be tucked out of sight or a misspelled word soon to be corrected in proofs. I'm not quite sure where to place this inscrutable genius of the place within the painting's gallery of phenomenological, ontological, and epistemological absorption. He personifies not only absorption, but excretion as well, embodying a whole economy of production in his scatological being. And the fruit of his labor, so to speak, is the quintessence of unsignificance, for waste, like poor Icarus, falls "unsignificantly" into a world of signs. A very bad planet indeed, my *kakkertje* poses the most unsignificant of insults to the beholder of his pictured world. Once you see him, it becomes hard not to think of the painting as "Landscape with Defecating Man."

In visual terms, we can think of the unsignificant as what we look at but do not see. Like my *kakkertje*, it may avoid our gaze—but the unsignificant sees *us*, or through us, in an uncanny sort of way. In this respect, the defecating man resembles another famous figure from the history of visual art. "This is how one pictures the angel of history," Walter Benjamin writes of Paul Klee's *Angelus Novus*:

His face is turned toward the past. Where we perceive a chain of events, he sees one single catastrophe which keeps piling wreckage upon wreckage and hurls it in front of his feet. The angel would like to stay, awaken the dead, and make whole what has been smashed. But a storm is blowing from Paradise; it has got caught in his wings with such violence that the angel can no longer close them. This storm irresistibly propels him into the future to which his back is turned, while the pile of debris before him grows skyward. This storm is what we call progress.

The angel of history faces the storm that blows him backward into the future. The defecating man, too, turns his back on history—the generations of viewers, including you and me, who glimpse him in the gallery and sail calmly on—even as his own gaze is forever absorbed by the material armature of the canvas that envelops him. He expresses no interest whatsoever in the "catastrophe which keeps piling wreckage upon wreckage" before Benjamin's hapless angel. He has no desire to "make whole what has been smashed." Far from it. Always already a litter bug par excellence, the *kakkertje* makes his little contribution to the pile of debris, supremely indifferent toward the storm we call progress. I don't know what to make of him. I can't even say if he exists or not. It puts me in an awkward position. The defecating man makes me self-conscious about my own forms of absorption in art, and in the world. Maybe that's why he's there, or not there, or somewhere in between.

LIKE A VERY STRANGE
LIKENESS AND PINK

I. THE LIKE

Let's kick things off with a little psychiatric evaluation. If I'm going to lecture on likeness for the next hour or so, I'd like to know what sort of people I'm dealing with. So make yourselves comfortable, please. I'm going to show you an image.

Take your time, and write down what it looks like to you. Rest assured, your responses will *not* be entered into your permanent record.

The Swiss psychiatrist Hermann Rorschach developed his famous inkblot test during the flowering of psychoanalysis in early twentieth-century Europe. As a child, Rorschach's classmates called him "Klecks," or "Inkblot," for his hobby of dripping ink onto a piece of paper, folding it in half, and opening the page to reveal the fanciful mirror images inside. Reading Freud on dream interpretation years later, the impossibly handsome Klecks began to wonder why people saw so many *different* likenesses—a butterfly, a monster, a volcano—in the *same* inkblots. He began to show inkblots to schoolchildren, analyzing their responses in what would become *Psychodiagnostik*, the book that introduced the Rorschach test to the world.

Psychologists ask their patients to look at inkblots as a "projective" test of personality. It's called a *projective* assessment because the subject, viewing an amorphous object—an inkblot, a cloud formation, a Swiss psychiatrist's hairstyle—projects their unconscious conflicts or motivations onto the form.

I, for one, can't help seeing a crashing tsunami in Klecks's hyperkinetic mane—but maybe that's just me. I'm an avoidant neurotic with low-order anxieties about male-pattern baldness and catastrophic weather events. Did you, by any chance, happen to see a spaceship in our original inkblot? In this respect, you're not unlike my six-year-old daughter—a Napoleonic introvert with a *Mars Needs Moms* complex—who insists it's "a rocket ship coming out of hot lava trying to kiss someone with little, little commas everywhere." Or maybe you saw a pair of dancers clasping hands in this phenomenological grey area instead? Then you have something in common with Hermann Göring—the man who brought us the Gestapo—who thoroughly enjoyed perusing the inkblots presented to him by prison psychiatrists at Nuremberg:

> [Laughs.] Those are two dancing figures, very clear, shoulder here and face there, clapping hands. [Cuts off bottom part with hand, including red.] Top red is head and hat; face is partly white.

Now that you know what it looked like to Göring, you might feel a little uneasy about seeing those dancers in the inkblot. Don't worry, my wife saw them, too, and she assures me, frequently, that she's *not* a Nazi. Though it's hardly foolproof as a psychiatric assessment, Rorschach's test sheds light on what might be called our folk psychology of likeness. For reasons beyond us, we feel that we're like others who perceive the same resemblances we do—and we also feel an ineluctable inkling of difference from those who don't recognize the likenesses we project onto the inkblot of the real.

Poets trade in resemblances—between things in the world, and between themselves and others—whenever they compose a simile. Is the news like squirrels? Am I the only person out there who feels like the news resembles squirrels? Will others see this likeness like *me*? Emily Dickinson—who once observed how "the news, like Squirrels, ran"—worried herself over these questions like nobody else in modern American poetry. Probably it has something to do with this poet's sense that she was utterly unlike the people around her. (In a letter to her literary pen pal Thomas Wentworth Higginson, the reclusive Dickinson once described herself as "the only Kangaroo among the Beauty.") In #723, she makes art of this anxiety:

Have any like Myself
Investigating March,
New Houses on the Hill descried—
And possibly a Church—

That were not, We are sure—
As lately as the Snow—
And are Today—if We exist—
Though how may this be so?

Have any like Myself
Conjectured Who may be
The Occupants of these Abodes—
So easy to the Sky—

'Twould seem that God should be
The nearest Neighbor to—
And Heaven—a convenient Grace
For Show, or Company?

Have any like Myself
Preserved the Charm secure
By shunning carefully the Place
All Seasons of the Year,

Excepting March—'Tis then
My Villages be seen—
And possibly a Steeple—
Not afterward—by Men—

Dickinson's uncertainty—"Have any like Myself"—lurks under the surface of every original simile. Have any, like myself, thought the news runs like squirrels? Sometimes, alas, the answer is no. I, for one, have no idea *what* this poet sees on her investigations into March. (Clouds—my best guess—appear "easy to the Sky" all through the year, and not only in spring.) Is that community on the hill real, or a hallucination? What doctrine do they preach in its possible church? Venturing beyond the boundaries of her historical community, Dickinson spies a spectral society that no one else sees—like a solitary anthropologist conducting fieldwork on a vanishing tribe—in the hills of rural New England. It's a lonely poem, making the question of social likeness—"Have any like Myself"—into an unanswerable refrain. Maybe to see like this poet, you have to resemble a kangaroo.

The hyphenated prosody of #723 allows for the possibility that collective life is but a dream: "If We exist— / Though how may this be so?" Though she's often read as a metaphorical poet, studying Dickinson's *similes* can help us to map our imagined communities of resemblance. One of her most widely anthologized poems, #320, begins with a classic simile of American literature:

There's a certain Slant of light,
Winter Afternoons—
That oppresses, like the Heft
Of Cathedral Tunes—

Whenever I teach this poem, all my students agree—there *is* a particular angle of bleak winter light that weighs on the soul like church music. Rhetorically speaking, Dickinson leaves us little room for dissent. There's no "I" in this poem, only the unanimous "us" and "we": "Heavenly Hurt, it gives *us*— / *We* can find no scar, / But internal difference, / Where the Meanings, are." But what if—heaven forbid—you're one of those benighted souls who happens to *like* sacred music? People who feel exalted by "Cathedral Tunes" might feel that Dickinson's first-person plural "oppresses" *them*. Though it looks universal at first, this simile selectively addresses itself to a secret society of like-minded agnostics who only pretend to sing along during church services in Dickinson's nineteenth-century Congregationalist community. Fans of sacred music may *crash* the simile, but they don't really belong to the poem's inner circle. Every likeness is a social occasion.

Now might be a good time to review a few basic principles from Simile 101. (Feel free to take notes; there will be a quiz.) Every simile, *The Princeton Encyclopedia of Poetry and Poetics* tells us, is composed of a tenor and a vehicle. The tenor is the thing itself: an inkblot, Hermann Rorschach's hair, a certain slant of light. The vehicle is what you, the poet, bring to the table: dancing imps, an approaching tsunami, the heft of cathedral tunes. Put them together in a wavy equation, and you have a simile:

TENOR		VEHICLE
Inkblot	≈	Dancing Imps
Rorschach's Hair	≈	Tsunami
Slant of Light	≈	Cathedral Tunes

But there's a paradox hidden inside any literary comparison. To liken one thing to another, your vehicle has to be recognizably *different* from its tenor. Imagine what would happen if Dickinson's poem began something like this:

> There's a certain Slant of light,
> Winter Afternoons—
> That oppresses, like the Heft
> Of a certain Slant of light,
>
> Winter Afternoons . . .

This vehicle doesn't travel very far, does it? To get any mileage out of her simile, Dickinson must liken winter's light to something *unlike* it. This "internal difference" at the heart of every simile is "Where the Meanings, are." (We'll return to the question of difference a little later in this talk.) For now, here's my unsolicited advice to students in Driver's Ed and Beginning Poetry Workshops: a good vehicle transports the reader as far as possible from its neighboring tenor. But sometimes a vehicle can spin out of control.

Though she ultimately refused to travel beyond her father's gate, Dickinson tricks out some of the most outlandish vehicles in the English language. She's like a gear freak at the auto show of resemblance. Let's look at a few examples. Take out your pencils, and see if you can supply these Dickinsonian vehicles with suitable tenors of your own. Print clearly. No talking, please. Extra credit for artful prosody:

TENOR		VEHICLE
_____	≈	a Panther in the Glove

_____	≈	Let of Snow
_____	≈	intermittent Plush
_____	≈	Chariots—in the Vest

OK, so what's like a panther in the glove? Any guesses? How about a let of snow? Intermittent plush? No, they aren't the titles of Steely Dan albums, though they really ought to be. Chariots in the vest, anyone? Sorry, time's up. Here are Dickinson's original similes, with the missing tenors supplied:

> It is simple, to ache in the Bone, or the Rind—
> But Gimblets—among the nerve—
> Mangle daintier—terribler—
> *Like a Panther in the Glove*—
>
> (#242)

★

> A Voice that alters—Low
> And on the ear can go
> *Like Let of Snow*—
>
> (#254)

★

> A Dog's belated feet
> *Like intermittent Plush*, be heard
> Adown the empty street—
>
> (#617)

★

The eager look—on Landscapes—

As if they just repressed

Some secret—that was pushing

Like Chariots—in the Vest—

(#696)

This is a totally unfair learning assessment, I know. My dictionary tells me "Gimblet" isn't even a word anymore. (Dickinson's talking about gimlets, the carpenter's tool for boring holes in wood, and not the gin cocktail, FYI.) But once you see how nerve pain feels "like" a panther in the glove—or how a low voice sounds "like" a let of snow, or how a dog's paws pad down the street "like" intermittent plush, or how landscapes seem to hold secrets that surge "like" chariots thundering in your vest—you see things a little differently. Dickinson's literary comparisons make us perceive likenesses like someone *unlike* us. For a spell, we behold the world like kangaroos amid the beauty. That's the unsung work of this venerable trope. Every memorable simile increases the communal fund of likeness available within a society.

Occasionally, a poetic vehicle achieves escape velocity, leaving its tenor behind entirely. "It scatters like the Birds— / Condenses like a Flock— / Like Juggler's Figures situates / Upon a baseless Arc." Like the birds, like a flock, like juggler's figures—we find plenty of vehicles aloft here, but where on earth is the tenor? When Dickinson sent these cryptic verses to an editor at the publishing house Roberts Brothers, she supplied the answer in the poem's title: "Snow." A vehicle without a tenor is a kind of riddle. At her most philosophical, Dickinson *never* reveals the answers to her riddles—"The Riddle we can guess / We speedily despise," writes this literary Sphinx—in order to foreground the mystery of likeness itself. In one of Dickinson's signature poems, the riddle remains unsolved to the end:

It was not Death, for I stood up,
And all the Dead, lie down—
It was not Night, for all the Bells
Put out their Tongues, for Noon.

It was not Frost, for on my Flesh
I felt Siroccos—crawl—
Nor Fire—for just my marble feet
Could keep a Chancel, cool—

And yet, it tasted, like them all,
The Figures I have seen
Set orderly, for Burial,
Reminded me, of mine—

As if my life were shaven,
And fitted to a frame,
And could not breathe without a key,
And 'twas like Midnight, some—

When everything that ticked—has stopped—
And space stares—all around—
Or Grisly frosts—first Autumn morns,
Repeal the Beating Ground—

But, most, like Chaos—Stopless—cool—
Without a Chance, or spar—
Or even a Report of Land—
To justify—Despair.

This "it" is the ultimate inkblot. Dickinson might be hinting at her theological sense of perdition, or the historical trauma of civil war, or some domestic contretemps with a family member, or internal difference itself.

(Maybe it's all of the above.) Riddled with doubt, the poet won't say what "it" is, but she can tell us what it *isn't*. The parade of negative definitions that opens the poem—it's not death, not night, not frost, nor fire—dramatizes metaphor's failure to solve the riddle of human feeling. "And yet," Dickinson writes, "it tasted, *like* them all." Her poem works like a rudimentary algorithm, first trying out various metaphors for "it," then feeding the recycled vehicles (death, night, frost, fire) into simile's wavy equation. With each iteration, we come closer to finding an apt likeness for "it"—progressing from "some" like in the fourth stanza to "most" like in the sixth—in this methodic poem of sequential approximations.

Just when we expect to learn what "it" is *most* like, though, Dickinson's riddle jumps off the tracks. We began with failed metaphors of death, night, frost, and fire. Then three of these metaphors—death, night, and frost—return as similes: "The Figures I have seen / Set orderly, for Burial, / Reminded me, of mine"; "'twas like Midnight, some"; "Or Grisly frosts." But something weird happens just when we expect Dickinson's fourth metaphor, fire, to come down the poem's conveyer belt: a new and entirely *different* vehicle usurps fire's position in the final stanza. Oddly, we learn that "it" is "most, like *Chaos*—Stopless—cool." What happened to fire? Fire isn't cool, and it isn't stopless, either. (It's hot, and it burns out, by its very nature.) Entering a new kind of variable into her lyric algorithm, Dickinson enters a lineage of poets from Hesiod to John Cage who've sought literary forms for chaos since time immemorial. Ovid places it at the outset of his epic cosmogony:

> *Ante mare et terras et quod tegit omnia caelum*
> *unus erat toto naturae vultus in orbe,*
> *quem dixere chaos.*

Before the sea and the earth and the all-covering sky
nature appeared the same throughout all the world,
which men called chaos.

Once upon a time, everything was one thing: "unus erat toto naturae vultus in orbe." Chaos reigns in a world *without* differences. But we've seen how likeness, to exist, depends on some form of "internal difference" between vehicles and their tenors. Dickinson's "it," then, is "most like" something—chaos—that's ontologically beyond compare. Chaos is absolutely self-identical, inherently *unlike* anything else. To shore up this metaphysical contradiction, Dickinson immediately slips a hidden comparison into her poem's final lines. At bottom, Dickinson's version of chaos looks a lot like the sea: "Without a Chance, or spar— / Or even a Report of Land— / To justify—Despair." Maybe "Despair" is the answer to Dickinson's riddle. It's not death, night, frost, or fire. But it tastes like them all.

II. THE UNLIKE

Historically speaking, efforts to give chaos any kind of form end badly. The largely forgotten Maestro Bartolomé's early modern Venn diagram of chaos seems too orderly by far when you look at it today. That's probably why it's largely forgotten. Half a millennium later, the Japanese artist Takashi Murakami's super-flat *Chaos* looks like a kindergarten cupcake party gone horribly awry.

You could call Murakami's image *Childhood* or *Death* or *Internal Difference*—any number of things could replace *Chaos* as the picture's title—

and I'd buy the resemblance. Leafing through art archives for chaos's true likeness is enough to justify despair, believe me. But sometimes I think Modernism came pretty close.

Like Dickinson's version of chaos, Pablo Picasso's painting is "stopless"—try tracing the snarled labyrinth of lines in the picture's lower left quadrant—and "cool," with its mellow palette of earth pigments: beige, ecru, khaki, olive, tobacco, and umber. Unlike the Murakami or the Bar-

tolomé, this image doesn't look "like" anything in particular at first. Picasso once described a painting as a "sum of destructions." Forget what you learned in Cubism 101, and this canvas resembles nothing so much as a crumpled sheet of old parchment retrieved from the dustbin of art history, smoothed out, and framed for exhibition.

Does Picasso's Cubist inkblot look like anything to *you*? In an essay with the memorable title "The Art of the Day after Tomorrow," from a collection with the even more memorable title *I Know Everything*, the French journalist Jacques de Gachons describes his first encounter with this image:

> The well-intentioned layman is a bit like the turkey in the fable: he definitely sees something, but he's not sure what it is.
>
> The young and sympathetic dealer [Daniel-Henry Kahnweiler] comes to my aid: "Oh! I know that the reading of Picasso's and Braque's most recent works is quite difficult. Of course it's easier for me; I was there when the paintings were done. I know all about what the artist wanted to put in them. For instance, monsieur, this one represents *The Poet*."
>
> "Ah!" (Good manners demand that I limit the expression of my total astonishment to this exclamation. I thought I was looking at a landscape, and it turned out to be a poet.)

The know-it-all de Gachons can be forgiven for mistaking this portrait for a landscape. (The turkeys in La Fontaine's fable aren't so lucky: they fall prey to a fox because they fail to recognize what they're looking at.) Personally, I can't help but see a Turneresque scene in the fish-scale wavelets of brushwork, the outline of a ship's prow and sail, and the scribbled atmospheric dusk of the picture's left margin. But once you focus your attention on the rounded crown and sloping profile at the top of the canvas, a peculiar likeness begins to take shape around this poet's cranium. See those overlapping corners that indicate the backrest of his armchair? A little clay pipe projects from his mouth at a jaunty angle. You can make out his hands, too, grasping a rolled-up manuscript at bottom center.

Now that we know what we're *supposed* to see in this 131.2 × 89.5 cm region of unlikeness, let's have a closer look at our poet's head. Or maybe I should say "heads." In this Cubist portrait's radical economy, Picasso offers us two countenances for the price of one. The left-facing profile resembles an African sculpture—maybe one from Picasso's private collection—underscoring the poet's otherness. The domed brow, intent gaze, and pursed lips lend this racialized hemisphere of his identity an air of fierce command, like the ruler of some sub-Saharan kingdom. On the other hand, his right-facing conjoined twin looks a little melancholy to me, invisible eyes downcast, mouth vaguely indexed by that chalky pipe. There's something of a sad kangaroo to this aspect of the poet; he seems to be perpetually mourning his own self-difference. "A head," Picasso once said, "is a matter of eyes, nose, mouth, which can be distributed in any way you like." In this distribution of the sensible, however, certain commodities appear to be in short supply; the poet's discordant profiles must make do with a single moustache, like interfused Mr. Potato Heads from a toddler's nightmare. No wonder our two-faced subject isn't feeling like himself forever.

Of course, nobody—unless they're chaos personified—can ever be wholly self-identical, when you think about it. We all feel like fierce African kings and sad, pipe-smoking kangaroos from time to time. So why does Picasso call this painting *The Poet*, and not *Everyman*, or *Self-Portrait*, or *Hermann Rorschach*? Poets look just like anyone else on the outside, after all. It's some kind of "internal difference" that distinguishes them from others, as Dickinson knew, maybe all too well. To truly depict his subject, Picasso needs to show us what's *inside* a poet's head.

What do we see here? Amid the chaos of drifting glyphs—a listing crucifix, the remains of a reversed swastika—one pictorial motif emerges intact. Whenever I look at this painting, I can't help but see a steeply sloped pyramid—its translucent apex piercing an ochre banner like a parody of the Great Seal on the back of the US dollar bill—embedded in the poet's cranium. There's even a little patch of sky in the offing. It could be a background detail plucked out of Hieronymus Bosch, or an eruption of proto-Surrealism in one of Klecks's inkblots. Have any, like myself, seen this tomb in the poet's head? I can't find any reference to it in the literature on Picasso's painting. Maybe it's just me—I'm a delusional thanatophile with pharaonic inclinations. But I hope you might see it, too. Gazing on this archaeological will-o'-the-wisp, I know how Dickinson felt when she glimpsed that imagined community—"and possibly a Steeple"—unseen by others.

Anyone who majored in English in the '90s knows that it's always already never a good time to review basic concepts from Post-Structuralism 101. But Jacques Derrida, the last century's great rhapsode of differences, might help us to unlock this miniature pyramid entombed in the poet's skull. In a 1968 address to the French Philosophical Society, Derrida spells out his thoughts on what he calls *différance*. The clown prince of grammatology coined this theoretical neologism by replacing the penultimate *e* in the French word for "difference" (*différence*) with an *a*. It's a devious sleight of hand, really, because you can't hear any difference between the original *e* and Derrida's interpolated *a* in spoken French. You can only *see* it:

> It is read, or it is written, but it cannot be heard. It cannot be apprehended in speech, and we will see why it also bypasses the order of apprehension in general. It is offered by a mute mark, by a tacit monument, I would even say by a *pyramid*, thinking not only of the form of the letter [*A*] when it is printed as a capital, but also of the text in Hegel's *Encyclopedia* in which the body of the sign is compared to the Egyptian Pyramid. The *a* of *différance*, thus, is not heard; it remains silent, secret and discreet as a tomb.

Like Derrida's undercover *a*, the pyramid inside the poet's head is "silent, secret and discreet as a tomb"—but I, for one, can't help *seeing* it nonetheless. Once glimpsed, it's as inescapable as the tomb, too. Traditionally, artists picture a poet's difference from others by crowning the head with a laurel wreath.

Importing his Cubist sign of unlikeness into the poet's head, Picasso psychologically frames it as an "internal difference." Poets look just like everybody else on the outside, yes, but they make a different kind of sound. That pyramid in the skull pictures that different sound. Picasso's portrait isn't a poet's likeness, exactly. It's an *unlikeness*.

III. THE NOT UNLIKE

Sometimes when I despair of making any sense in this lecture, I imagine sitting in the audience for Derrida's talk about *différance*. Throughout the published version of his speech, the theorist ties himself into knots to make clear when he's discussing *différence* versus *différance*, which sound exactly the same in French, but mean entirely different things. To be honest, I've never understood the difference between "difference" and *différance* myself. But that sneaky little *a* is the key. In this respect, it's not unlike the "A" that opens Gertrude Stein's literary portrait of Bernard Faÿ:

A is an article.

"A" *is* an article—grammatically speaking—most of the time. A portrait, a poem, a sad kangaroo. But it's also a noun: the alphabetical character *a*. Pronounce it as a short vowel, and you have an article, while a long *a* gives voice to a noun. The two *a*'s look identical on paper, but they sound different. Stein's *a*, then, is the hermeneutical mirror image of Derrida's *a*. One is seen but not heard, while the other is heard but not seen. Unlike the philosopher, this poet doesn't try to spell out *différance*—she *sounds* it out.

Fashioning likenesses from sound instead of paint makes perfect sense if you're suspicious of visual appearances. The sitter for Stein's portrait, Bernard Faÿ, was obsessed with discerning invisible differences between people; under the Vichy regime, he was responsible for sending hundreds of suspected Jews and Freemasons to German concentration camps. Might there be a dark side to Stein's Modernist sound portraiture? Barbara Will's 2011 book *Unlikely Collaboration* illuminates the historical complexities of Stein's involvement with the Fascist regime as a Jewish writer living in occupied France. A "Jew" or a "Freemason" may look just like anybody else on the outside. So can a poet, or a homosexual, or a sacred music aficionado, for that matter. Stein's sound portraits echo-locate individuals within the imagined communities of her time, just as

Dickinson's musical vehicle—"Cathedral Tunes"—distinguishes believers from agnostics in her Congregationalist social order. For the silent heretic in Amherst, and for the queer Jewish poet under a Nazi collaborator's patronage, "*internal* difference" is "where the Meanings, are."

Over the course of nearly half a century, Stein composed some of the most peculiar likenesses in the history of Western portraiture. Her sound portraits reimagine the figure and ground of art, resemblance, and identity itself. Now let's turn from Stein's portrait of the infamous Faÿ to another example of poetic unlikeness in her work. Can you echolocate *this* famous historical subject? (It isn't a Hermann—either Rorschach or Göring—if that helps to narrow the field.) Think of this as our final exam.

If I told him would he like it. Would he like it if I told him.

Would he like it would Napoleon would Napoleon would would he like it.

If Napoleon if I told him if I told him if Napoleon. Would he like it if I told him if I told him if Napoleon. Would he like it if Napoleon if Napoleon if I told him. If I told him if Napoleon if Napoleon if I told him. If I told him would he like it would he like it if I told him.

Now.

Not now.

And now.

Now.

Exactly as as kings.

Feeling full for it.

Exactitude as kings.

So to beseech you as full as for it.

Exactly or as kings.

Shutters shut and open so do queens. Shutters shut and shutters and so shutters shut and shutters and so and so shutters and so shutters shut and so shutters shut and shutters and so. And so shutters shut and so and also. And also and so and so and also.

Exact resemblance to exact resemblance the exact resemblance as exact as a resemblance, exactly as resembling, exactly resembling, exactly in resemblance exactly a resemblance, exactly and resemblance. For this is so. Because.

Now actively repeat at all, now actively repeat at all, now actively repeat at all.

Have hold and hear, actively repeat at all.

I judge judge.

As a resemblance to him.

Who comes first. Napoleon the first.

Who comes too coming coming too, who goes there, as they go they share, who shares all, all is as all as as yet or as yet.

Now to date now to date. Now and now and date and the date.

Who came first Napoleon at first. Who came first Napoleon the first. Who came first, Napoleon first.

Presently.

Exactly do they do.

First exactly.

Exactly do they do too.

First exactly.

And first exactly.

Exactly do they do.

And first exactly and exactly.

And do they do.

At first exactly and first exactly and do they do.

The first exactly.

And do they do.

The first exactly.

At first exactly.

First as exactly.

As first as exactly.

Presently

As presently.

As as presently.

He he he he and he and he and and he and he and he and and as and as he and as he and he. He is and as he is, and as he is and he is, he is and as he and he and as he is and he and he and and he and he.

Can curls rob can curls quote, quotable.

As presently.

As exactitude.

As trains.

Has trains.

Has trains.

As trains.

As trains.

Presently.

Proportions.

Presently.

As proportions as presently.

Father and farther.

Was the king or room.

Farther and whether.

Was there was there was there what was there was there what was there was there there was there.

Whether and in there.

As even say so.

One.

I land.

Two.

I land.

Three.

The land.

Three

The land.

Three.

The land.

Two

I land.

Two

I land.

One

I land.

Two

I land.

As a so.

They cannot.

A note.

They cannot

A float.

They cannot.

They dote.

They cannot.

They as denote.

Miracles play.

Play fairly.

Play fairly well.

A well.

As well.

As or as presently.

Let me recite what history teaches. History teaches.

Who is *he*? "He he he he," writes the poet, as if she were laughing at the very question. This line's phonemic "he" only assumes the dimensions of a full-blown grammatical and psychological subject when it's followed by "is": "He is and as he is." Pronounced as a series of spondees, "he he he he" sounds like sardonic laughter; but the unstressed "he" of "he is and as he is" invokes a man. Like the "A" that opens "Bernard Faÿ," parts of speech assume new ontologies when they're voiced differently in this poem. We see, and *hear*, this ambiguity in the lexicon of "resemblance" Stein mobilizes throughout her portrait: "like," "as," and "so." "So" can act as an adverb or a conjunction, depending on when and how you say it. "As" functions variously as an adverb, a conjunction, or a preposition. "Like" works the hardest of all, moonlighting as an adverb, a conjunction, a preposition, an adjective, a verb, or a noun. I can't think of another word in our language that's like "like" in this respect. The poem's opening question—"If I told him would he like it"—exploits this diversity of meaning to subtly stress the connection between pleasure and resemblance. Will he like his likeness? It all depends on who he is. "Napoleon" would be a reasonable guess, but that's *too* exact a resemblance for Stein's elliptical art. Napoleon surfaces in this portrait because he's not unlike the diminutive yet commanding subject of the poem: "If I Told Him, A Completed Portrait of Picasso."

Stein, like Picasso, makes portraits that show how likeness itself is not what it seems. To some readers, "If I Told Him" may resemble nonsense—a form of linguistic chaos—but I think it's more like one of Rorschach's inkblots when you look closely enough at it. Unlike chaos, Stein's repetitions are never self-identical. When "exactly as as kings" becomes "exactly or as kings," the almost imperceptible difference of phrasing—from *as* into *or*—casts any "exact resemblance" whatsoever into doubt. (Micro-variations of this sort can be read as markers of difference *or* similarity throughout Stein's work.) It's worth keeping in mind that "exactitude as kings" is a pluralized, and not an absolute, sovereign. By the end of the poem, it's hard to say whether "a note" is like or unlike "a float" with *any* exactitude. Are we talking about a musical note or a doctor's note? A parade float, or a root beer float? Stein's rhyme makes us hear how "a note" resembles "a float" in the realm of sound, though they may be quite different in other ways. Sound, then, establishes an invisible network of resemblance throughout Stein's portrait of Picasso. Because a note afloat sounds like "they dote," we sense the invisible relationship between musical movement and desire. Two lines later, "They as denote" introduces *meaning* into the wavy equation. Somehow it makes perfect sense that this series of rhymes concludes with the line "Miracles play." Stein is a poet in the ecstatic tradition, if you take her at her word. Her verbal portraits awaken us to unseen orders of resemblance.

In the end, I can't really say whether Stein fills her literary canvas with internal differences or internal resemblances. Are shutters *like* queens? What's the difference between asking "If I told him would he like it" and "Would he like it if I told him"? Is "now" the same thing when it appears three lines after another "now"? Maybe we can think of these things as *not unlike*. Of course, the double negative is only a more roundabout way of saying that something is "like" another. But it's different, too. Stein's portraits produce a comparative field of the not-unlike in literary art. Is it just me, or are there political ramifications to this way of seeing resemblances? On any given day, I'm not sure if I'm like a Freemason, or different from a Freemason. But after gazing on Stein's inkblot of Bernard Faÿ, I'd proudly say, "I'm not unlike a Freemason." (For the record, I'm totally not a Freemason—but you get the idea.) What would our imagined communities look like if this were our measure of affiliation? They might resemble utopias, or chaos. I think Stein wants us to consider the possibilities. By the end of "If I Told Him," we find ourselves in a history lesson. "Let me recite what history teaches," the poet concludes. "History teaches." How is a portrait like a history lesson? We've just come in from recess, where our teacher reminded us to "play fairly." Or maybe it was music class, where we managed to "play fairly well." Is the music room like a playground? Is a poem like a painting? Stein's experiments in resemblance show us how different things are not unlike. She makes portraits of objects, landscapes of plays, and geographies of identity. Everything, in her words, is "like a very strange likeness and pink."

WONDER: A SYZYGY

I. THE WORLD WORLDS

It's probably not the most promising beginning to this talk for me to observe that my subject, like silence, has a way of disappearing the moment you speak of it. Love, anger, regret, even boredom—wonder's antipodes —may entrench themselves in us more deeply over time, but wonder, I'd venture, is always already a fugitive affair. Maybe it's a matter of developmental psychology; in the middle of life, I find myself becoming a nostalgist of childhood wonder. (These days I feel it mostly in my dreams.) Or maybe it's civilization itself that's outgrown its wonder years. We start out with the marvels of the ancient world—the Great Pyramid of Giza, the Hanging Gardens of Babylon, the Colossus of Rhodes—only to arrive, in our disenchanted era, at Wonder Bread. Any way you slice it, wonder is ever vanishing. Still, I suspect the occasional sighting of this endangered affect has something to do with why someone like me continues to write poems in the twilight of the Anthropocene. Of course, William Wordsworth said all this more eloquently and in pentameter verse, too. Maybe poetry is a faint trace of wonder in linguistic form. By following that trace for the next hour or so, I hope we'll come a bit closer to wonder itself.

Let's begin with an early wonder of the Western literary tradition. In Book 18 of the *Iliad*, the god Hephaestus forges a shield for Achilles, who's lost his armor in the bloody fog of war. But as Hephaestus works the shield's surface, this peculiar blacksmith—being a god, after all—simply can't resist creating a world, too:

> There he made the earth and there the sky and the sea
> and the inexhaustible blazing sun and the moon rounding full
> and there the constellations, all that crown the heavens

A little creation myth blossoms amid the slaughter, as Hephaestus hammers not only the Earth but—within the brief passage of three dactylic hexameters—the totality of the known cosmos onto the shield as well. And he's only just getting warmed up, really. Over the next hundred and fifty lines of the poem, Hephaestus emblazons the shield's surface with a compact survey of ancient civilization, including the arts of war, law, agriculture, animal husbandry, astronomy, music, dance, and so on. A sensualist at heart, he sets this panorama buzzing all over with Epicurean minutiae: we see "bunches of lustrous grapes in gold, ripening deep purple"; we hear a boy plucking his lyre, "so clear it could break the heart with longing"; we even taste the savor of "a cup of honeyed, mellow wine." Not bad for a piece of antiquated military equipment. Faced with such artistry, I can't help thinking of the shield's disabled maker as a kind of poet, like the blind Homer himself. Sure enough, Hephaestus incorporates a miniature epic into the shield's pageantry, too, with its own besieged city, fraught war councils, interfering gods, and loved ones watching anxiously from the ramparts as a tiny surrogate Hector is hauled "through the slaughter by the heels." No wonder Homer describes the shield as "a world of gorgeous immortal work." It contains an entire *Iliad* and more within its gilt compass.

Beguiled by Homer's art, some readers have even tried to reverse engineer *real* shields from this literary blueprint over the millennia. Probably the most spectacular example of all time was fabricated for display at George IV's coronation banquet by the sculptor, draftsman, and Homer enthusiast John Flaxman in 1821. It's a marvel of nineteenth-century British punctiliousness in low relief.

Here we find bunches of lustrous grapes in gold, a boy with his lyre, and that cup of honeyed wine—all meticulously accounted for. And yet I can't help feeling this luminous artifact offers, at best, only a low-resolution copy of the Homeric original. Let's zoom in for a moment on those golden hounds at their masters' feet to have a closer look.

I'm not sure why Homer enumerates the figures in this little tableau with such exactitude amid all the shield's armies, crowds, and processions—"and the golden drovers kept the herd in line, / *four* in all, with *nine* dogs at their heels"—but it offers us a perfect opportunity to check Flaxman's work for quality control. Four drovers? Check. Now let's count the dogs. (You might think *I'm* being persnickety here, and with good reason, but bear with me just a little longer.) So where *is* that ninth hound? Marianne Moore once famously claimed that "omissions are not accidents." It's hard to say whether Flaxman's missing hound is an omission or an accident, but it makes me wonder.

Listen carefully and you'll hear the poor beast—"barking, cringing away"—somewhere in the vaporous limbo between fiction and reality. "Paws flickering," it's a creaturely cipher for what's lost when we translate the virtual into the real. The artist, former US Army cryptographer, and Homer enthusiast Cy Twombly illustrates this loss in oil, crayon, and graphite in his postmodern *Shield of Achilles* a century and a half later.

You won't find our missing hound here, either—and that's the whole point of Twombly's abstraction. All those kinetic scribbles convey Homer's *energeia*, or literary energy, but they also make an absolute hash of the shield's pictorial imagery. Not even a cryptographer can code so much world into so small a space. Whether you reconstruct it like Flaxman or deconstruct it like Twombly, the shield of Achilles will forever remain an impossible object. It belongs to that wondrous category of things that are larger inside than outside, like a poem, or a person, or a world. "The world is not the mere collection of the countable or uncountable, familiar and unfamiliar things that are at hand," writes Martin Heidegger in *The Origin of the Work of Art*, "but neither is it a merely imagined framework added by our representation to the sum of such given things. The *world worlds*." Homer's shield isn't a picture of all the countable or uncountable things—star systems, ripening grape clusters, flickering hounds—that populate the world. As Flaxman and Twombly discovered, it can't even be pictured at all. But it *worlds*.

"Glorious armor shall be his, armor / that any man in the world of men will marvel at / through all the years to come," Hephaestus predicts as he hammers the glowing cosmos on his forge. If you were to survey the readers' responses to this literary marvel over the millennia—from the anonymous commentators of antiquity to moderns like Alexander Pope and G. E. Lessing to undergraduate term papers in HUM 101—you'd end up with something like a brief history of wonder in Western civilization. Describing the plowmen at work on the shield's figured surface, Homer himself is the first among mortals to express wonder at its construction:

> And the earth churned black behind them, like earth churning,
> solid gold as it was—that was the wonder of Hephaestus' work.

I can't imagine a more gorgeous description of humanity's passage through the dark field of world: "the earth churned black behind them, like earth churning." But why doesn't Homer say the shield's golden *surface* churned like earth churning? This Möbius strip of a simile is a marvel in its own right. Spellbound by Hephaestus's artistry, we forget the shield's a shield in the first place—so we *feel* we're watching soil behave "like" itself. It's a kind of reverse alchemy, where gold becomes dirt, vehicle becomes tenor, and shield becomes world. Sometimes it seems there's no *escaping* wonder before such worlding work. Of the golden women depicted in the shield's wedding procession, Homer writes: "Each stood moved with wonder." I'm not sure whether we should envy or pity these embossed figures, forever frozen in transport at the wonder they inhabit.

But there's a serious glitch in the god's plans for this "world of gorgeous immortal work." Though Hephaestus prophesies that "any man in the world of men will marvel" at his craft, *none* of the many men in the *Iliad*—Trojan or Greek—ever marvel at the shield's construction. Achilles's fellow soldiers won't even look at the god's radiant work: "none dared / to look straight at the glare, each fighter shrank away." Only a blind genius could invent such tragic optics. Homer embeds a gilded cosmos in the midst of the epic for his readers to marvel at through the ages, but the *Iliad*'s inhabitants remain forever blind to this wonder hidden in plain view. Beholding his gift from the gods, even Achilles— the only mortal who scrutinizes the shield's figured surface—fails to wonder at the sight:

> The more he gazed, the deeper his *anger* went,
> his eyes flashing under his eyelids, fierce as fire—
> exulting, holding the god's shining gifts in his hands.

Rage [*mēnis*] is the first word of the *Iliad*, and we usually associate it with blindness rather than perception: "I was blinded, lost in my inhuman rage," says Agamemnon during one of his many changes of heart in the poem. But Homer envisions something like a *phenomenology* of rage in this scene: "The more he gazed, the deeper his anger went." For Achilles, anger is more than affect—it's an adjunct of perception itself. Only once he's "thrilled his heart with looking hard / at the armor's well-wrought beauty" does he break off his furious gaze. Instead of blinding him, rage furnishes this exceptional character with a singular perspective on things.

Why does Achilles alone rage at this "world of gorgeous immortal work"? It may have something to do with his sense of vocation. In Book 9 of the *Iliad*, we find him in his tent, "plucking strong and clear on the fine lyre" he won in battle long ago, "singing the famous deeds of fighting heroes." I can't help feeling this armchair bard would have made a passable poet in a different world. (Isn't every poet a sulky egotist with a hyperactive death drive, after all?) But Achilles is born to fight, not to sing. Anything that comes between him and his bloody vocation—including the "beautifully carved" lyre, "its silver bridge set firm"—must be cast aside for him to follow this calling. Not even life itself matters more to him than this grim occupation. "'Hard on the heels of Hector's death *your* death / must come at once,'" his mother warns him, but Achilles only retorts, "'Then let me die at once.'" What's the point of living if you can no longer kill? Achilles doesn't work to live, he lives to work— Homer uses the word *ergon*, which means something like "labor," to describe the hero's exertions on the battlefield—and his business is death.

Wonder, for the Greeks, led to a very different sort of vocation. We see this illustrated in a scene from Plato's *Theaetetus*, where Socrates plays his customary role of career counselor to a youth he's interrogated to the point of utter perplexity:

THEAETETUS: By the gods, Socrates, I am lost in wonder when I think of all these things, and sometimes when I regard them it really makes my head swim.

SOCRATES: It seems that Theodorus was not far from the truth when he guessed what kind of person you are. For this is an experience which is characteristic of a philosopher, this wondering [*thaumazein*]: this is where philosophy begins and nowhere else.

Funny how Theaetetus must first become "lost in wonder" in order to *find* himself. He learns "what kind of person" he is—a philosopher—from his brush with *thaumazein*. This beats any aptitude test I took in high school. For Plato, wonder "is where philosophy begins and nowhere else." No wonder, no philosophers. Even Aristotle, who built a whole philosophical system from his lover's quarrel with Plato, agrees on this point. "It is through wonder that men now begin and originally began to philosophize," he observes in the *Metaphysics*, "wondering in the first place at obvious perplexities, and then by gradual progression raising questions about the greater matters too, *e.g.* about the changes of the moon and of the sun, about the stars and about the origin of the universe." If this sounds familiar, it's because we've come full circle, to the origin of the cosmos—the Earth, the stars, "the inexhaustible blazing sun and the moon rounding full"—that Hephaestus hammered onto the shield's bright circumference in the first place. But we've yet to consider those "greater matters" that form the astronomical rungs on the ladder of Aristotle's ascent into *thaumazein*—the moon, the sun, the stars, and the origin of the universe. Let's take the next step in wonder's philosophical progression, and look to the moon.

Sooner or later, the moon pops up on pretty much every poet's literary horizon. Whether you're a Japanese courtesan, a Yoruban folk singer, or a Conceptualist cosmonaut, it's as close as the art comes to a timeless universal motif. But how many poets ever make the moon feel *new* in their art? Nearly 350 years ago, John Milton managed to work a nifty little lunar renovation into the epic paraphernalia of *Paradise Lost,* as the irrepressible Satan—after nine days and nights in free fall from the battlefield of heaven—takes up arms once again:

> His ponderous shield,
> Ethereal temper, massy, large and round,
> Behind him cast. The broad circumference
> Hung on his shoulders like the moon whose orb
> Through optic glass the Tuscan artist views
> At evening from the top of Fesolè,
> Or in Valdarno to descry new lands,
> Rivers or mountains in her spotty globe.

Even the most pious poet can't resist a bit of literary vandalism now and then. Emblazoning the full moon on Satan's shield, Milton blots out the classical world of Achilles's shield—just as *Paradise Lost* will, he hopes, eclipse the *Iliad* in the annals of literary history someday. "Massy" yet also "ethereal [in] temper," Satan's shield is another kind of impossible object, or hyperobject. It belongs to that wondrous category of things that hold dual citizenship in the realms of the material and the ideal, like a poem, or an angel, or the venerable moon itself. Since antiquity, astronomers had speculated about the moon's ontology—was it composed of ethereal vapors, or massy like the Earth?—until Milton's "Tuscan artist" put these theories to the proof with the aid of his "optic glass." Oddly, we don't really *see* much of the moon on Satan's shield. Superimposed on its "spotty globe," we find a portrait of Galileo Galilei—the man in Milton's moon—who, more than any poet or rebel angel, revolutionized our view of the heavens above.

Milton visited Galileo—by then old, blind, and under house arrest—in Florence during the summer of 1638. (DreamWorks has been sitting on my script of this story for *ages*.) In his book *The Starry Messenger*, Galileo had published the first topographical drawings of the moon's surface to appear in the West nearly three decades earlier.

Peering through his telescope, the Florentine astronomer marveled at a cratered and mountainous terrain that defied expectation:

> The surface of the Moon is not even, smooth and perfectly spherical, as the majority of philosophers have conjectured that it and the other celestial bodies are but, on the contrary, rough and uneven, and covered with cavities and protuberances *just like the face of the Earth*, which is rendered diverse by lofty mountains and deep valleys.

Galileo discovered that the moon, too, was a world, "just like" ours. Look closely at that progression of topological nouns ending Milton's lines and you'll see how the moon came of age as a world in this period—from a flat "circumference" to a volumetric "orb" to a mapmaker's "globe." In Galileo's wake, the French engraver Claude Mellan's moon maps would soon highlight the chiaroscuro curvature of the lunar orb.

By the end of the eighteenth century, the moon had assumed world-like dimensions in the British artist John Russell's aureate globe.

All this time, Earth was yielding its last blank spots—known as sleeping beauties—to the epistemological imperium of geography. But now another "spotty globe" offered "new lands, / Rivers or mountains" to be mapped—and the moon was only the beginning.

The moon on Satan's shield heralds a revolution in the history of cosmological wonder. Galileo's telescope revealed a host of worlds in the heavens above—new moons circling Jupiter, stars never before seen by the human eye—all swiftly incorporated into blind Milton's literary vision of the cosmos. *Paradise Lost* stages a universal masque of wonder beneath this canopy of plural worlds. Awestruck, Adam delivers a Hamletic soliloquy on outer space, which makes of "this earth a spot, a grain, / An atom with the firmament compared / And all her numbered stars that seem to roll / Spaces incomprehensible." Milton himself wonders if God might "ordain / His dark materials to create more worlds" from chaos someday. Satan, too, plays the amateur cosmologist, speculating that "space may produce new worlds" for his legions to invade following their expulsion from the kingdom of heaven. If you find *Paradise Lost* slow going, try reading it as science fiction. (Spielberg, what are you waiting for?) Nebulous monsters wing their way through star systems. Angels and demons alike imagine humans colonizing other planets. For the first time in English poetry, we view the Earth from outer space—"that globe whose hither side / With light from hence though but reflected shines"— half cloaked in brightness, half in shadow. I could go on. But amid all this, the archangel Raphael warns Adam—and, consequently, Star Trek aficionados everywhere—to "dream not of other worlds, what creatures there / Live in what state, condition or degree." Maybe wonder, like the moon, has a dark side.

Let's not forget that the most wonderstruck character in *Paradise Lost* also happens to be the most fiendish by far. Unlike furious Achilles, Satan simply can't stop mooning over all of creation. From the stairway to heaven, he "looks down with wonder" at the Earth below; once he's touched down on our planet, he gazes upon Eden "with *new* wonder"; when he first sees Adam and Eve, he's overcome by "wonder and could love" them, too. Such vulnerability to wonder, on Satan's part, is frankly *endearing*. I, for one, can't help feeling sympathy for the poor devil when we last see him—at the conclusion of his final speech to the rebel angels in hell—still wondering to the bitter end:

> He stood expecting
> Their universal shout and high applause
> To fill his ear when cóntrary he hears
> On all sides from innumerable tongues
> A dismal universal hiss, the sound
> Of public scorn. He *wondered* but not long
> Had leisure, *wond'ring at himself* now more:
> His visage drawn he felt to sharp and spare,
> His arms clung to his ribs, his legs entwining
> Each other till supplanted down he fell
> A monstrous serpent on his belly prone

I've felt this way after poetry readings myself sometimes. (Isn't every poet a narcissistic angel in reptilian form, after all?) Satan's ultimate object of wonder in *Paradise Lost* isn't a newly discovered planet, or humankind, but "himself," transformed into a serpent. You'd expect Satan to feel *horror* at this grotesque Ovidian metamorphosis—his cranium warping hideously, his arms fusing into his torso, his legs corkscrewing into a scaly tail—but this anti-hero's wondrous journey through the cosmos ends where it began, in a failure to see himself for what he really is. Maybe dreaming too much of worlds beyond reach can make a monster of you.

Worlds swim through *Paradise Lost* like bubbles in a glass of champagne, but Milton cautions us not to lose sight of ourselves in this teeming universe. Who's more blind to our world than the astronomer squinting into his telescope's eyepiece? "They can foresee a future eclipse of the sun," writes Augustine in his *Confessions*, "but [they] do not perceive their own eclipse in the present." I suspect Milton had this sort of *inner* eclipse in mind when he described Satan's dusky radiance following the archangel's fall from heaven:

His form had not yet lost
All her original brightness nor appeared
Less than archangel ruined and th' excess
Of glory obscured, as when the sun, new ris'n,
Looks through the horizontal misty air
Shorn of his beams or *from behind the moon*
In dim eclipse disastrous twilight sheds
On half the nations and with fear of change
Perplexes monarchs. Darkened so, yet shone
Above them all th' archangel

Milton's selenographic shield may advertise Galileo's discoveries, but its spotty globe also reminds us that Lucifer—the erstwhile "bringer of light"—is, in truth, eclipse personified: "Darkened so, yet shone / Above them all th' archangel." Nothing discloses the dark side of wonder like an eclipse. I once saw one, through a piece of welder's glass, in a derelict park on the other side of the world. Even the crows seemed perplexed by its disastrous twilight. There was an uncanny chill, as if a refrigerator door had swung open inside me. But the wonder of it all wasn't that the sun had been blotted out overhead. What stopped my breath was the slow silhouette of another world gliding into view.

III. WORLDS WITHIN

Three centuries after *Paradise Lost* first lit up the Western literary firmament, an American poet, cookbook author, and marijuana enthusiast named Ronald Johnson purchased an 1892 edition of Milton's poem in a Seattle bookshop—and promptly began to black out most of the text from its pages.

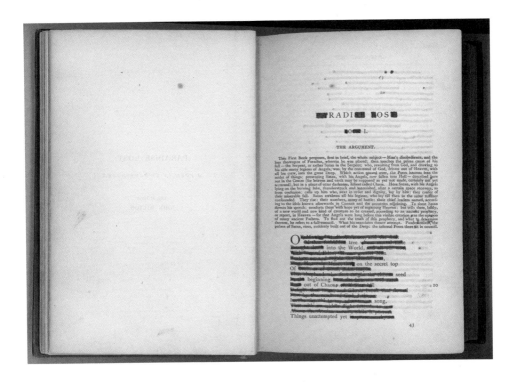

Why would anyone so meticulously deface an already outdated copy of the venerable Puritan epic? "I got about halfway through it, kind of as a joke," Johnson later explained in an interview, like a sheepish delinquent caught spray-painting a cathedral. "But I decided you don't tamper with Milton to be funny. You have to be serious." What began as a little joke at Milton's expense developed into a postmodernist masterpiece of literary eclipse in its own right. Blot out the first and last two letters of "paradise," and you have "radi." Lose the first and last letters of "lost," and you have "os." Even the title of the poem Johnson fashioned from this procedure—*Radi Os*—is ordained solely from Milton's dark materials.

Before publishing this literary curio, Johnson scrupulously *whitewashed* the epic he'd defaced, yielding a photographic negative of his poetic eclipse:

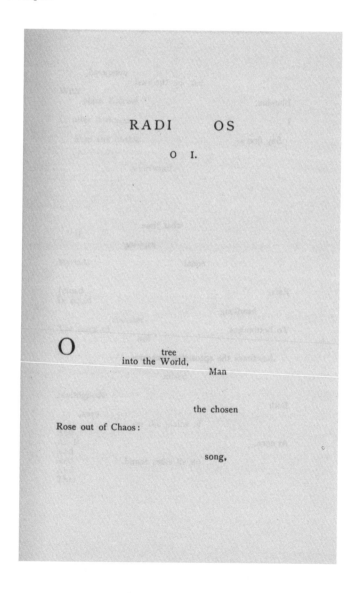

Nobody wrote *Radi Os*. The poem was wondrously *erased* into existence. Its author's words are nowhere to be found in this work, and yet—like Milton's Creator—he's everywhere.

"There is another world," the French poet Paul Éluard once said, "but it is inside this one." I think Johnson would gently amend this to say there are other *worlds*, but they are inside this one. Turning the astronomical theater of *Paradise Lost* inside out, Johnson investigates the plurality of worlds *within*: "worlds, / That both in him and all things, / drive / deepest." A little textual puzzle from *ARK*, the cosmological epic Johnson labored over for twenty years, illustrates the wondrous multiplication of inner worlds throughout this poet's work:

> earthearthearth
>
> earthearthearth
>
> earthearthearth

The literary critic Stephanie Burt has deciphered the secret messages embedded in this triple-decker concrete poem. Earth, earth, earth. Ear, the art hearth. Hear the art, hear the art. Sampling a jeremiad from the King James Bible—"O earth, earth, earth, hear the word of the Lord"—Johnson composes a manifold *matrix* of worlds (and hearts). It's one thing to register the "verse" in "universe," and another entirely to construct a poetics of the multiverse. The erasurist's decision *not* to delete the "s" that pluralizes his book's title makes worlds of this difference. *Radi Os* isn't a radio, it's an *orchestra* of radios. Well, that's not quite right. See that caesura fracturing the poem's title? An imaginary number of *broken* "radi os" hums and buzzes inside this literary hyperobject. One radio may tune into a single frequency at a time, but a chorus of broken radios can broadcast everything from an infernal racket to the music of the spheres all at once. "You don't tamper with Milton to be funny," our holy fool may attest, but for all its radical theology, *Radi Os* is, in the end, a divine musical comedy.

Listen carefully, and you'll hear a marvelously cracked piece of post-modern music playing behind the curtain of Johnson's literary erasure. At a party with his students one night—so the story goes—the poet first heard a recording of *Baroque Variations* by the composer Lukas Foss. At one point in the work, a xylophone spells out "Johann Sebastian Bach" in Morse code. Elsewhere, a highly trained musician smashes a bottle with a hammer. Johnson's various enthusiasms must have lined up nicely that evening, because he embarked upon the "solitary quest in the cloud chamber" that would become *Radi Os* the very next day. In the dedicatory note to his book, Johnson quotes Foss's liner notes for "Variation I" —on a larghetto by Handel—as a sort of key to his own work:

> Groups of instruments play the Larghetto but keep submerging into inaudibility (rather than pausing). Handel's notes are always present but often inaudible. The inaudible moments leave holes in Handel's music (I composed the holes). The perforated Handel is played by different groups of the orchestra in three different keys at one point, in four different speeds at another.

Handel's larghetto, from the Concerto Grosso, op. 6, no. 12, may very well be the most beautiful melody the composer ever wrote. It's easy enough to find online, if you'd like to hear the "always present but often inaudible" original music behind Foss's *détourned* "Variation I" sometime. Then listen to the Foss, and you'll experience the otherworldly beauty of Handel under eclipse. It's hard *not* to hear broken radios searching for a classical music broadcast in this perforated larghetto's eerie harmonics and bursts of sonority. If you find *Radi Os* slow going, try reading it as the libretto for a post-structuralist space opera—lyrics erased by Johnson, score perforated by Foss.

The wonder of variations—in music, in poetry, in evolutionary biology, and elsewhere—is how one variation begets another, though you never know what you'll beget. Perforating *Paradise Lost*, Johnson produced a literary variation on Foss's musical variation on a Baroque artist who composed dozens of variations of his own—including Hephaestus's favorite, "The Harmonious Blacksmith." To see how *Radi Os* makes possible even further variations on itself, let's look at the original passage in the 1892 edition of *Paradise Lost* on the page where Satan's shield first appears.

Receive thy new possessor — one who brings
A mind not to be changed by place or time.
The mind is its own place, and in itself
Can make a Heaven of Hell, a Hell of Heaven.
What matter where, if I be still the same,
And what I should be, all but less than he
Whom thunder hath made greater? Here at least
We shall be free; the Almighty hath not built
Here for his envy, will not drive us hence: 260
Here we may reign secure; and, in my choice,
To reign is worth ambition, though in Hell:
Better to reign in Hell than serve in Heaven.
But wherefore let we then our faithful friends,
The associates and co-partners of our loss,
Lie thus astonished on the oblivious pool,
And call them not to share with us their part
In this unhappy mansion, or once more
With rallied arms to try what may be yet
Regained in Heaven, or what more lost in Hell?"   270
    So Satan spake; and him Beëlzebub
Thus answered: — "Leader of those armies bright
Which, but the Omnipotent, none could have foiled!
If once they hear that voice, their liveliest pledge
Of hope in fears and dangers — heard so oft
In worst extremes, and on the perilous edge
Of battle, when it raged, in all assaults
Their surest signal — they will soon resume
New courage and revive, though now they lie
Grovelling and prostrate on yon lake of fire,   280
As we erewhile, astounded and amazed;
No wonder, fallen such a pernicious highth!"
    He scarce had ceased when the superior Fiend
Was moving toward the shore; his ponderous shield,
Ethereal temper, massy, large, and round,
Behind him cast. The broad circumference
Hung on his shoulders like the moon, whose orb

Through optic glass the Tuscan artist views
At evening, from the top of Fesolè,
Or in Valdarno, to descry new lands,   290
Rivers, or mountains, in her spotty globe.
His spear — to equal which the tallest pine
Hewn on Norwegian hills, to be the mast
Of some great ammiral, were but a wand —
He walked with, to support uneasy steps
Over the burning marle, not like those steps
On Heaven's azure ; and the torrid clime
Smote on him sore besides, vaulted with fire.

What if somebody other than Johnson—say, a young woman in rural
New England on a snowy night long ago—were to compose her own
holes in this dark material?

                                                      time

     Can

          thunder

  Here
  Here   in my

   unhappy mansion

68

                    but

                       that voice

        Of

                                          fire

               scarce   ceased
                              the
        Ethereal

                                     artist

                          in her   globe

        Of

                          marle   steps
        On   and
               on

It's hardly "Because I could not stop for Death," but you get the idea.
There are *innumerable* poems encrypted in the "harmonious numbers"

of *Paradise Lost*. I even hear echoes of the sadly underrated poet, Star Trek aficionado, and Ronald Johnson enthusiast Srikanth Reddy in this literary cloud chamber.

           The mind is

               a

           matter

                                          my

                                               friends

                                 of

                          voice

                            the   edge

Of   it

                    moving

                                    like
                glass

            in
        Rivers

                                    but

            burning

I could do this forever, and that's exactly the point. You could, too. I suspect that's why Johnson breaks off his own work at Book 4 of *Paradise
Lost*, leaving nearly 7,000 lines of pristine Miltonic pentameters for others to cross out someday. "*Radi Os* kind of wrote itself," said the author
of this unfinished erasure. "I think it ended when it needed to end and I
didn't need to add the rest." An open-ended variation on Milton's song,
Radi Os invites *us* to "add the rest." And why stop at *Paradise Lost*, for
that matter? Compose your own holes in any book—*Alice's Adventures in
Wonderland*, the Constitution of the United States of America, *The Unsignificant*—and you'll unearth a manifold matrix of worlds within.

   A literary multiverse, *Radi Os* is riddled with cosmological worm-
holes, theological rabbit holes, and typographical holes. From the "O
tree," a slant rhyme for *poetry* that opens the work, to the "O for / The
Apocalypse" that trumpets the poem's closing revelations, Johnson

makes us *see* the "hole" in "whole" and *hear* the "hole" in "holy." There's a hole in wonder, too, though I'd never tumbled through it until I came across the following page in *Radi Os*:

RADI   OS

A mind   to be changed by place or
                        lace
                Heaven of Hell,

            astonished on the oblivious pool,

            the O

Of

    wonder,

                                circumference
        Hung on   shoulders like the moon, whose
                optic glass
        At evening, from the top
                        new
                                globe

        Of some great

                burning
                    azure ;
                            vaulted

The first time I read this passage, I had no idea what lay behind it. But that floating little phrase—"the O / Of / wonder"—kept looping around in my head, so I dug up an old copy of *Paradise Lost* to read the Miltonic original, and was wonderstruck. Almost three thousand years ago, a blind Greek poet pictured the world on an ancient shield. Two and a half millennia later, the moon spied through an optic glass eclipsed Homer's world in a theological poem of Reformation England. In my own lifetime—I was four, astronauts had set foot on the moon's surface only a few years earlier—a little-known American poet erased Milton's spotty globe all the way down to a wondrous *O*. World, moon, *O*. The word for when things line up in this way is *syzygy*. The microscopic linkage of chromosomes necessary for reproduction in our species is one example. An eclipse—when three celestial bodies line up in astronomical space— is another. The word *syzygy* is itself a syzygy, which almost makes me believe in intelligent design as far as language is concerned. Read aloud its sequence of three identical vowels lined up in a row—*y, y, y*—and you'll hear humankind grappling with the mystery of causation. Let's not overlook that linked chain of *o*'s in "the O / Of / wonder," either. It's a syzygy, too. Why, why, why? Oh, oh, oh. We all live that song.

So many images flicker through this "O" in *Radi Os*—a full moon, a ghostly shield, a hole in a page from a timeworn edition of *Paradise Lost*— but I always return to a mouth open in wonder. When we see golden acrobats turning handsprings on an ancient shield, or when the mountains of the moon first swim into focus through a telescope's eyepiece, we say "O," hardly aware that our lips are assuming the shape of the signifier itself. The "O" *of* wonder, Johnson shows us, is the "o" *in* wonder. I can't think of any other word where our writing system and the morphology of human speech enter into such wondrous alignment. But the mouth forms an O in arousal, and in hunger, and in death's terminal rictus, too: "Thy mouth was open," George Herbert says to Death personified, "but thou couldst not sing." There's no such thing as pure or simple wonder. When *thaumazein* forces our lips into an O, all those ancient drives— from *eros* to *thanatos*—move through us as well. The art of poetry traditionally originates in this inexhaustible, sonorous O. O muse, O Lord, O my love, O late capitalism, O etcetera—the "O" that Johnson plucks out of wonder invokes endless poetic variation. With all due respect to Plato and Aristotle, philosophy isn't the only vocation that springs from *thaumazein*. If you look closely at the O of wonder, you'll see a poem beginning there, too.

SELECTED BIBLIOGRAPHY

AND WORKS CITED

Allart, Dominique. "*La chute d'Icare* des Musées des Beaux-Arts de Belgique à Bruxelles." *Art&Fact* 15 (1996): 104–7.

Aristotle. *The Metaphysics: Books I–IX*. Translated by Hugh Tredennick. London: William Heinemann, Ltd., 1933.

Auden, W. H. *Collected Poems*. Edited by Edward Mendelson. New York: Vintage, 1991.

Auden, W. H., and Christopher Isherwood. *Journey to a War*. London: Faber and Faber, 1939.

Augustine. *Confessions*. Translated by Henry Chadwick. Oxford: Oxford University Press, 1991.

Benjamin, Walter. *Illuminations: Essays and Reflections*. Translated by Harry Zohn. Edited by Hannah Arendt. New York: Harcourt, Brace & World, 1968.

Burnyeat, Myles. *The Theaetetus of Plato*. With a translation of Plato's *Theaetetus* by M. J. Levett. Indianapolis: Hackett Publishing Company, 1990.

de Tolnay, Charles. "Studien zu den Gemälden Pieter Bruegel d. Ä." *Jahrbuch der kunsthistorischen Sammlungen in Wien* 8 (1934): 110.

Derrida, Jacques. *Margins of Philosophy*. Translated by Alan Bass. Chicago: University of Chicago Press, 1982.

Dickinson, Emily. *The Poems of Emily Dickinson*. Edited by R. W. Franklin. Cambridge: Belknap Press of Harvard University Press, 1998.

Fried, Michael. *Absorption and Theatricality: Painting and Beholder in the Age of Diderot*. Berkeley: University of California Press, 1980.

Galilei, Galileo. *Galileo's Sidereus Nuncius, or, A Sidereal Message*. Translated by William R. Shea. Sagamore Beach, MA: Science History Publications, 2009.

Heidegger, Martin. *Basic Questions of Philosophy: Selected "Problems" of "Logic."* Translated by Richard Rojcewic and André Schuwer. Bloomington: Indiana University Press, 1994.

Herbert, George. *The Works of George Herbert*. Hertfordshire: Wordsworth Editions, 1994.

Homer. *The Iliad*. Translated by Robert Fagles. New York: Viking, 1990.

Johnson, Ronald. *ARK*. Edited by Peter O'Leary. Chicago: Flood Editions, 2013.

———. *Radi Os*. Berkeley, CA: Sand Dollar, 1977. Chicago: Flood Editions, 2005.

Karmel, Pepe. *Picasso and the Invention of Cubism*. New Haven: Yale University Press, 2003.

Merleau-Ponty, Maurice. *Phenomenology of Perception*. Translated by Donald A. Landes. Abingdon, UK: Routledge, 2012.

Milton, John. *Paradise Lost*. Edited by Gordon Teskey. New York: W. W. Norton, 2005.

Milton, John, David Masson, and Nathan Haskell Dole. *The Poetical Works of John Milton*. Boston, New York: T. Y. Crowell & Co., 1892.

Nemerov, Alexander. "The Flight of Form: Auden, Bruegel, and the Turn to Abstraction in the 1940s." *Critical Inquiry* 31, no. 4 (Summer 2015).

Picasso, Pablo, and Christian Zervos. "Conversation avec Picasso." *Cahiers d'Art* 10:10 (1935): 173–8. Reprinted in: Barr, Alfred H., Jr. *Picasso: Fifty Years of His Art*. New York: The Museum of Modern Art, 1946.

O'Leary, Peter. "An Interview with Ronald Johnson." *Chicago Review* 42, no. 1 (1996).

Ovid. *Metamorphoses*. Edited by R. J. Tarrant. Oxford: Oxford University Press, 2004.

Stein, Gertrude. *Dix Portraits*. New York: David Zwirner Books, 2022.

———. *Gertrude Stein: Selections*. Edited by Joan Retallack. Berkeley: University of California Press, 2008.

Stein, Leo. *Appreciation: Painting, Poetry, and Prose*. Lincoln: University of Nebraska Press, 1996.

Williams, William Carlos. *The Collected Poems of William Carlos Williams: Volume II, 1939–1962*. Edited by Christopher MacGowan. New York: New Directions, 2001.

Wittgenstein, Ludwig. *The Wittgenstein Reader*. Edited by Anthony Kenny. Oxford: Blackwell Publishing, 2006.

Zillmer, Eric A., Molly Harrower, Barry A. Ritzler, and Robert P. Archer, eds. *The Quest for the Nazi Personality: A Psychological Investigation of Nazi War Criminals*. Hillsdale, NJ: Lawrence Erlbaum Associates, Publishers, 1995.

The audio recording of Gertrude Stein's "If I Told Him, A Completed Portrait of Picasso" is available on the Poetry Foundation's website: www.poetryfounda tion.org/podcasts/76509/if-i-told-him-a-completed-portrait-of-picasso

ACKNOWLEDGMENTS

The Bagley Wright Lecture Series on Poetry supports contemporary poets as they explore in depth their own thinking on poetry and poetics and give a series of lectures resulting from these investigations.

This work evolved from lectures given at the following institutions and organizations: "The Unsignificant" at the Library of Congress, Washington, DC, September 10, 2015; "The 'O' of Wonder: a Syzygy" at Counterpath at University of Denver, Denver, CO, September 18, 2015; "The Unsignificant" at New York University, New York, NY, October 2, 2015; "The Unsignificant" at Princeton University, Princeton, NJ, October 5, 2015; "The 'O' of Wonder: a Syzygy" at Yale University, New Haven, CT, October 7, 2015; "The 'O' of Wonder: a Syzygy" at University of California, Berkeley, Berkeley, CA, October 22, 2015; "Like a Very Strange Likeness and Pink" in collaboration with the New Writers Project and the Harry Ransom Center at University of Texas at Austin, Austin, TX, November 5, 2015; "Like a Very Strange Likeness and Pink" at the University of Arizona Poetry Center, Tucson, AZ, November 19, 2015; "Like a Very Strange Likeness and Pink" at Seattle Arts & Lectures, Seattle, WA, December 1, 2015; "The Unsignificant" at the Poetry Foundation, Chicago, IL, December 3, 2015.

Thank you to Rob Casper, Matthew Blakley, and Anya Creightney at the Library of Congress; Julie Carr and Tim Roberts at Counterpath; Soren Stockman at New York University; Cate Mahoney at Princeton University; Langdon Hammer at Yale University; Jane Gregory at University of California, Berkeley; Lisa Olstein at University of Texas at Austin; Tyler Meier, Hannah Ensor, and Sarah Kortemeier at the University of Arizona Poetry Center; Rebecca Hoogs at Seattle Arts & Lectures; Steve Young at the Poetry Foundation; and all of their respective teams, for welcoming the Bagley Wright Lecture Series into their programming and for collaborating on these events. The Series would be impossible without such partnerships.

"The Unsignificant" appeared in *BOMB* 168. An excerpt from "Like a Very Strange Likeness and Pink" appeared in *Poetry* 224, no. 5.

tion. Galileo's moon sketch courtesy of Linda Hall Library of Science, Engineering & Technology. *Three representations of the moon* by Claude Mellan, courtesy of The Elisha Whittelsey Collection, The Elisha Whittelsey Fund, 1960. *Radi Os* images courtesy of the Ronald Johnson Collection, Kenneth Spencer Research Library, University of Kansas. Used with permission of the Literary Estate of Ronald Johnson.

NOTE FROM THE AUTHOR

Sometimes acknowledgments are hard to tell from apologies—to anyone who left one of these lectures scratching their heads, thank you for not leaving earlier.

Likewise my gratitude, for your patience among other things, to my good friends at Wave Books—I can't imagine a more luminous home for these ruminations.

Thank you, and sorry, to anyone I've neglected to name here.

And thanks, for everything, to my wife and daughter, Suzanne and Mira, who carried on without me while I traveled to deliver these talks over the autumn of 2015. Thank you to my father-in-law, Frank, for everything and more. This book is for you.